The Bad Boys of Diplomacy

translated
by S. Novikov

ABOUT THIS BOOK

The first part of this book describes the behaviour of that "special" category of drivers who have diplomatic privileges on the roads of various countries. You'll read answers from the Ministries of Foreign Affairs of 22 countries: Vatican, Great Britain, Switzerland, Singapore, Poland, Norway, New Zealand, Moldavia, Malaysia, Luxembourg, Lithuania, Liechtenstein, Kazakhstan, Ireland, Georgia, Finland, Denmark, Czech Republic, Croatia, Brazil, Bulgaria, and Armenia. These data have never been published before, and so some of the stories are quite incredible and shocking.

In the second part of the book we will talk about personae non gratae. Usually the motives for declaring someone a persona non grata are this diplomat's hostility towards the government of the state of residence, interference with its internal affairs, disrespect of its laws, customs etc.

The latest version of the book can be found at the following locations:
  www.amazon.com/dp/1530794048
  www.amazon.co.uk/dp/1530794048

Printed in the United States of America

ISBN-13: 978-1530794041
ISBN-10: 1530794048

The first part of this book describes the behaviour of that "special" category of drivers who have diplomatic privileges on the roads of various countries. Some of them drink & drive, some of them are guilty of speeding, and some just don't like to pay the parking fees. Amazingly, it is often not possible to prosecute them for this, and so the countries where these diplomats reside lose substantial amounts of money on fines alone.

So diplomats of which countries violate the law most often? And diplomats of which countries almost never violate the law? Which countries openly share statistics about foreign diplomats violations, and which countries conceal them? This book answers these questions and includes frank comments from the diplomats themselves that sheds light on the behavior of their colleagues from different countries.

You'll read answers from the Ministries of Foreign Affairs of 22 countries: Vatican, Great Britain, Switzerland, Singapore, Poland, Norway, New Zealand, Moldavia, Malaysia, Luxembourg, Lithuania, Liechtenstein, Kazakhstan, Ireland, Georgia, Finland, Denmark, Czech Republic, Croatia, Brazil, Bulgaria, and Armenia. These data have never been published before, and so some of the stories are quite incredible and shocking.

At the end you will also be able to clearly see who holds the top spots in law violation amongst the diplomatic corps.

In the second part of the book we will talk about personae non gratae. Usually the motives for declaring someone a persona non grata are this *diplomat's hostility towards the government of the state of residence, interference with its internal affairs, disrespect of its laws, customs etc. Often the phrase "for impermissible activities incompatible with diplomatic status" lurks behind it, which can also mean an espionage charge.*

Read on to find about about some fascinating details associated with this somewhat unpleasant status.

1.The list of diplomats-violators (from 22 countries):

1.1. This is information from the Ministry of Foreign Affairs of Poland

1.2. Here is the information from the Ministry of Foreign Affairs of Armenia, giving the police data

1.3. Here is the information from the Ministry of Foreign Affairs of Lithuania

1.4. Here is the official response of Vatican

1.5. Great Britain

1.6. Switzerland

1.7. Singapore

1.8. Here is another answer from Singapore

1.9. Norway

1.10. Another answer from Norway

1.11. New Zealand

1.12. Moldavia

1.13. Malaysia

1.14. Luxembourg

1.15. Liechtenstein

1.16. Kazakhstan

1.17. Ireland

1.18. Georgia

1.19. Finland

1.20. Here is another answer from the police of Finland

1.21. Denmark

1.22. Czech Republic

1.23. Croatia

1.24. Another answer from Croatia

1.25. Brazil

1.26. Bulgaria

2. The information on personas non grata (from 21 countries):

2.1. Lithuania

2.2. New Zealand

2.3. Norway

2.4. Slovenia

2.5. Republic of South Africa

2.6. Sweden

2.7. Switzerland

2.8. Great Britain

2.9. Ukraine

2.10. Bosnia and Herzegovina

2.11. Ireland

2.12. Georgia

2.13. Finland

2.14. Germany

2.15. Denmark

2.16. Cuba

2.17. Czech Republic

2.18. Canada

2.19. Columbia

2.20. Here is another response from Columbia

2.21. Belarus

2.22. Australia

The first part of this book presents the commentary obtained from various countries' ministries of foreign affairs on the following issues:

The problem of violation of traffic rules by drivers with diplomatic privilege has been reported repeatedly in the print media of numerous countries. Diplomat drivers are exempted from fines for violation of the rules of the road in accordance with Vienna Convention on Diplomatic Relations of 1961.

Thus, frequent and gross violations of traffic rules by diplomats in the country of their residence are a notion which fairly attracts the attention of journalists from all over the world.

It is also important to note that diplomats of a number of countries as a rule observe the rules of the road in the country of their residence, and in case of violation pay corresponding fines in time. Such practice of demonstrating respect for the laws of the country of residence (for an absolutely legal opportunity not to pay any fines) is worthy of respect.

1. Diplomats* of what countries violate the rules of the road and parking rules (without paying fines and parking fees, other kinds of obligatory payments) most often in your country? Please provide the information concerning 5-10 countries, diplomats of which failed to pay such fines and fees most often during the period of years 2010, 2011, and 2012.

---

*in accordance with articles 1 and 31 of Vienna Convention on Diplomatic Relations of 1961, "members of the diplomatic staff" and "diplomatic agents" belong to diplomats uncharged with responsibility in the country of residence

2. What kinds of traffic and parking rules violations are most often committed by diplomats residing in your country (exceeding of speed limit, illegal parking, drunk driving, etc.)? Please provide the information on the period of years 2010, 2011, and 2012.

3. Diplomats of what countries have not been reported to commit any traffic and parking rules violations in your country? Diplomats of what countries paid fines and other kinds of payment in corpore in case of violation of the rules of the road? Please provide the information of the period of years 2010, 2011, and 2012.

So let us get an insight into what different countries' ministries of foreign affairs think:

1.1. This is information from the Ministry of Foreign Affairs of Poland:

Dear Sir,

*In reply to your letter dated September 3, 2012, (no. DR4379) I would like to kindly inform you that the Polish Police **do not keep statistical records of traffic code violations committed by persons enjoying immunity under the Vienna Convention on Diplomatic Relations.** The Polish law does not provide for fining persons enjoying diplomatic privileges and immunities for traffic offences or for issuing them penalty points. The Police register only traffic violations with the involvement of foreign diplomats that result in a collision or an accident and cause an injury to persons or vehicles. The Police also do not breathalyse the drivers who are protected by diplomatic immunity.*

It should be highlighted that there are 95 diplomatic missions and 14 international organisations accredited to Poland with over 1500 vehicles registered on diplomatic license plates.

23 road collisions caused by the foreign diplomats or their family members have occurred to date in 2012. It should be noted that some Embassies have only one person staff, while others have as many as one hundred. Consequently, the number of the Embassy vehicles reflects the size of the Embassy staff. Missions whose staff has been responsible for more than one collision include: the United States of America (4 collisions), the Russian Federation, China and the Federal Republic of Germany – two collisions each.

Considering the number of staff of these missions, there

is no ground to maintain that their respective diplomats commit more traffic offences than diplomats from other states.

In 2011, 39 collisions were caused by diplomats or their family members. Most collisions were caused by the following Embassies: the United States of America (9 collisions), Russia (3 collisions), China, Iraq, Kuwait, Germany, Ukraine and Vietnam – 2 collisions each.

In 2010, the Police recorded 36 collisions caused by diplomats or their family members. The greatest number of collisions was caused by the Embassies of: the United States of America and France – 4 collisions each, Russia (3 collisions), China, Iran, Portugal, and Slovakia – 2 collisions each.

The most frequent causes of collisions are: exceeding speed limits, wrong manoeuvring (passing, turning, joining in traffic).

There are many Embassies whose staff has not been involved in any traffic collision in 2010-2012, among them are the following missions of the European countries: Albania, Armenia, Belarus, Croatia, Denmark, Greece, Georgia, Estonia, Finland, Lithuania, Luxembourg, Macedonia, Norway, Romania, Slovenia, the Holy See, Switzerland, Turkey, and the United Kindom.

I hope that the above information will prove useful in your professional work.

Best regards,
Michal Safianik
Director
Press Office

A diplomat commented the situation as follows:
You should not forget that a vast majority of violations goes unnoticed. The reason is that a car with a diplomatic number plate can easily leave a traffic accident scene and ignore the instructions of the local road inspection agencies.

An embassy worker on the list contributed:
Nobody is perfect! The severity of imperfection differs, though... When in Paris, a graffiti on the Forum wall caught my eye. It read, "All French people want equality; but everyone wants privileges..." Simple as it is, the maxim sums it up perfectly. The more imperfect one is, the farther off the normal track one gets. The most widespread (and the most innocent, too) traffic violation among diplomats when abroad is bad parking...

Here is another comment by a diplomat representing one of the listed countries:
As for drunk driving, this is rather an outrageous violation and everyone will find out about this through mass media. I cannot thing of a single incident hushed up, simply because people like "hot" news regardless of the country. Even if the diplomat is lucky enough to cause no damage to any people, he or she will surely be recalled. When it comes to speeding, I cannot give a specific answer... Sometimes it is a matter of office-related necessity, though such situations are rather infrequent. Failure to pay for parking seems the most complicated issue. Some governments disregard it and charge no fines, while others give parking tickets, which is obviously hopeless. In some countries,

diplomatic privileges do not cover parking. As a result, it is the traffic violator and not the diplomatic mission who is to pay.

I believe there are no psychological factors that contribute to it, just the specific mindset or mentality of the individual diplomat and not the country's diplomatic staff.

Diplomatic missions either denounce violations when trumpeted widely or give a silent response. They hardly ever engage in any disputes, since you can easily get stuck in this controversy for ages, totally unable to carry your point to the opponent.

As for unspoken rules, they are all spelled out in each country's traffic rules, non-compliance being actually a violation of law.

When it comes to explicit, or conscious, traffic violation "out of necessity) mostly speeding or forbidden maneuvering which does not interfere with other road users' activity), the cases are few and mostly justifiable. We should not neglect blatant provocative acts of the governments, which I believe to occur regularly.

A diplomat representing a non-violating country (as presented by Poland's Ministry of Foreign Affairs) has the following opinion:

The only right the diplomat has is to be a role model.

A diplomat explicitly violating generally accepted rules does the job poorly…

1.2. Here is the information from the Ministry of Foreign Affairs of Armenia, giving the police data:

Please find attached the Reference prepared for You by the Police of the Republic of Armenia, concerning your letter to the President of Armenia about diplomatic transport.

Please confirm the receipt of the email.
Best Regards,
Makar Melikyan

Ministry of Foreign Affairs of Armenia
Attaché at the Department of Press, Information and Public Relations

REFERENCE

In the Republic of Armenia 501 means of transport are registered belonging to embassies, consulates, international organizations and missions having diplomatic status, of which 127 belongs to administrative-technical service staff.

During 2010 the driver of the Embassy of France was held administratively liable be the traffic police officers for violating traffic rules (1 offense).

During 2011 there were no records of traffic rules violations with the involvement of vehicles registered on diplomatic license plates.

During 2012 traffic rules violations were only recorded through roads speedometer devices and cameras. Through these devices only in December 68 offences were disclosed. The highest number of the recorded offences was caused by the vehicles belonging to the following Embassies: Iran (14),

United States (10), Germany (8), China (6), Russia (6), France (6), Belarus (6), Georgia (3), Turkmenistan (3), Greece (2), Italy (1), India (1), Thailand (1), Romania (1) and Bulgaria (1).

The surveys of the above mentioned offences recorded through roads speedometer devices and cameras caused by diplomatic staff have been sent to the Ministry of Foreign Affairs of the Republic of Armenia to give diplomatic solution.

The vehicles belonging to the Embassy of Lebanon, Canada, Norway and Uruguay consulates have not been involved in traffic rules violations.

During 2010 and 2011 correspondingly a case of traffic accident was caused with the involvement of the vehicles belonging to the Embassy of The Russian Federation. As a result of the implemented proceedings the drivers were subjected to administrative liability.

During 2012 with the involvement of transport means of the Embassies of France (1), Russia (1) and German (1) a traffic accident was caused and in connection with these accidents administrative proceedings were not conducted. The vehicles belonging to U.S. and Iranian embassies were also involved in a traffic accident and as a result of implemented proceedings the driver of the Embassy of Iran was held administratively liable and the materials of administrative violations directed to the employee of the US Embassy according to Article 16 of the Administrative Offences Code of the RA were sent to the Ministry of Foreign Affairs.

Police of the Republic of Armenia

Here is the comment of a Russian diplomat:

Generally, the problem does exist with diplomats. They do violate traffic rules. A couple of years ago, they could hardly stop an African embassy's car in Moscow. It was a scandal. Such things happen to diplomats of very nearly all countries.

I have an experience of drinking driving, say, after receptions. You just have to take a sip of wine or whiskey at a reception. It is our job. There is no different way of acting under the conditions. I After all, you cannot leave the car!

Sober people can violate rules, too. Sometimes there are urgent orders that require immediate response. For example, one of your diplomats was involved in an accident or something like that. Sometimes you have to drive at a breakneck speed escorted by the local police. It does not happen too often, though.

When on a car trip, your senior manager might force you to violate traffic rules, although it is unnecessary.

Quite naturally, diplomatic immunity can go to one's head. Even the diplomatic corps is not free of irresponsible idiots. They are normal people, just like you and us!

By the way, European diplomats, especially those coming from Baltic, East European, and CIS, and Asian ones enjoy greater reverence and respect. It encourages diplomats coming from those countries to violate traffic rules. It is not uncommon for the US or Canadian police to be unaware of whether they are dealing with diplomats. They do not care who the offender is. It does nourish a sense of responsibility.

A diplomat whose friends are frequent traffic violators answers our questions:

What are the psychological triggers that make diplomats violate traffic rules in the host country?

There is a single trigger – a sense of permissiveness; a sense of having access to what is inaccessible in any other context. I am not going to tell you what wealthy European country it is, but one of our diplomats told me that they drove drunk occasionally in the evenings because they can.

How should the foreign ministries representatives of which violate traffic rules respond to such violations?

All violations are recorded by the police; these are reported to the embassy, which mostly confines its corrective measures to reprimanding. Flagrant violations, like those causing an accident, might bring about expulsion (persona non grata), which diplomats mostly find rather unattractive.

Can traffic violations be justified under certain conditions (office-related necessity; an obvious need to break frankly absurd restrictions)? Can you give an example of diplomatic driving of in other countries?

I think such justifying situations to be very few if any. Yet, what underlies the diplomatic immunity is meant to eliminate provocations and the like. Violations of the kind do occur periodically. However, they are of little significance when analyzed against the backdrop and negligible in most countries.

1.3. Here is the information from the Ministry of Foreign Affairs of Lithuania

MINISTRY OF FORIGN AFFAIRS OF THE REPUBLIC OF LITHUANIA INFORMATION AND PUBLIC RELATIONS DEPARTMENT

In response to your enquiry, we would like to inform you that the Ministry of Foreign Affairs of the Republic of Lithuania has been receiving enquiries from the Police Department under the Ministry of Interior about the owners of the vehicles with diplomatic number plates and the diplomatic immunity of the drivers. However, no statistics are kept on road traffic offences committed by persons driving the vehicles without diplomatic number plates.

Road traffic offences are almost often committed by drivers while being on duty and on the way to the meetings of events. Biggest part of those offences comprises exceeded speed limits.

Diplomatic missions and representations of 35 foreign countries and 9 international organizations are located in Vilnius with a total of 426 vehicles with diplomatic number plates.

In 2010 there were about 140 road traffic offences committed by persons driving the vehicles with the diplomatic number plates, 138 offences were committed in 2011, and 144 offences – in 2012. It should be noted that the vehicles were not always driven by diplomats themselves.

Director   Giedrius Puodžiūnas

An embassy employee's comment:

Of course, diplomats don't have to violate traffic rules. They just lack a sense of responsibility. Grown-up people, if you please, take a queer pleasure in it. I guess it often depends on the diplomat's personality and not on the country, agency, etc. In some countries, like the United States, it is really challenging to get a diplomatic job. Apart from useful contacts, one has to study hard and have an unblemished reputation. Unfortunately, the latter play little role in Russia if any. The Ministry of Foreign Affairs consists of those who have the useful contacts or MGIMO graduates who failed to get another job. Just like the army, a country's ministry of foreign affairs is greatly representative of its society.

Violations are unacceptable. Diplomatic status is meant not to encourage driving against traffic lights but to eliminate potential pressure on diplomats. The Convention was specifically developed in order to prevent pressure from host countries.

A Military Attaché's Assistant of one of the countries answers our questions:

What are the psychological triggers that make diplomats violate traffic rules in the host country?

The diplomat is human, after all! (Question mark). Not every diplomat is a diplomat (in fact, charity and diplomacy are the best covering activities ever). I graduated from the School of Foreign Military Information... Am I a military journalist, a translator? NO! I don't think we have the institution of young professional diplomats! Who wants to go to Burundi :)

where a new revolution breaks out every month? Everybody knows everybody in those hot countries... Even though I had a lot of useful contacts, I had to spend much time and effort to take root in a prosperous European country...

Looks like we have departed from the subject... I have given you the only answer possible. Diplomats are human, too.

Can traffic violations be justified under certain conditions (office-related necessity; an obvious need to break frankly absurd restrictions)? Can you give an example of diplomatic driving of in other countries?

I drive a car without a diplomatic number plate, but I might violate traffic rules, knowing that I would get away with that... I think it depends on the driver alone... Let me make a confession. I have sinned. I did drunk driving once. God was merciful to me, and the trip was trouble-free... That evening in Argenteuil (France), a drunk driver killed two children... I felt ashamed... because I could have been in his place!... Since then, I do not drive drunk... Just for the reference, there is no driver's position at the Embassy.

Here is the opinion of another diplomat:
The two major traffic violation triggers are impunity in diplomatic missions and drunk driving. When diplomats violate traffic rules, they leave the scene under the protection of their diplomatic mission to mispresent the accident to appear innocent using their contacts.

However, sometimes diplomats take public transport and emergency service lanes to avoid traffic jams (either out of necessity or just feeling reluctant to wait).

In Belgium, the police round up diplomatic traffic violators at weekends).

By the way, sometimes the reason underlying traffic violations is legal and other agencies being reluctant to deal with such offenders. Therefore, to solve this problem it is necessary to review the international standards, which would make appropriate measures to bring violators to justice possible. Specific methods should be adopted for detaining traffic violators should be developed for every country.

However, not all countries seem willing to disclose information related to diplomatic offences in their territory.

Many countries refuse to provide such information on a number of pretexts, though it would be helpful in minimizing diplomatic traffic violation.

The positive thing about the denials is that you can see which countries are prepared to share their lists of offenders, and which are being secretive.

1.4. <u>Here is the official response of Vatican:</u>

December 10, 2012

Dear Sir,
I'm referring to the questions you raised in relation to breaches of the Highway Code in Vatican City by members of the Diplomatic Corps.
The Vatican City is a small country with few, narrow and short roads controlled by the staff of the Gendarmerie, designed to control the traffic, so that the violations of the Highway Code are very limited.
The Diplomatic Corps has many spaces reserved for parking therefore, up today, no one has ever done to detect traffic violations against them and against their cars.
Sincerely

Office Command
Gendarmerie
Vatican City

1.5. Great Britain:

10 December 2012

Thank you for your letter dated 22 November 2012, to the Prime Minister, David Cameron, about the violation of rules of the road and parking rules by foreign diplomats in Great Britain. As Protocol Directorate of the Foreign and Commonwealth Office (FCO) leads on matters relating to the Vienna Convention on Diplomatic Relations 1961 (VCDR 1961) and because certain Articles of the VCDR pertain to respecting the laws and regulations of the receiving State (i.e. the United Kingdom) and diplomatic immunity I have been asked to reply.

Under Article 41 of the VCDR 1961, drivers entitled to immunity are not exempted from fines for violation of the rules of the road and are expected to obey the law. The FCO does not tolerate members of the diplomatic community breaking the law. We take all incidents of traffic violations seriously.

The Protocol Directorate, in conjunction with local authority boroughs, carries out an exhaustive investigation into traffic violation matters committed by the diplomatic community and the information is published in an annual report to Parliament. The report is readily available to the public. I attach a link to the most recent report for 2011, which should answer to your questions:

<u>*Lord Hansard text for 5 Jul 2012 (pt 0001)*</u>

The information that you have requested for the years 2010 can also be found by using the above link. The information that you seek for the year 2012 is presently being compiled.

Andy Palmer
Deputy Head, Diplomatic Missions and International Organisations Unit

1.6. Switzerland:

16 October 2012

Thank you for your interest. You find below our answer. Best regards. Pierre-Alain Eltschinger – EDA-INFO

Switzerland is a decentralised country in which the cantons have a large number of responsibilities and competences. As for fines imposed on diplomats working in Switzerland, there are no national statistics. The FDFA (the Swiss ministry of foreign affairs) has the figures for 2011-2012 in the canton Bern, where most embassies are located. These figures show that most fines were imposed for incorrect parking, followed by fines for speeding and for ignoring traffic lights. For reasons of data protection, the FDFA cannot provide details about the diplomatic representations involved.

Département fédéral des affaires étrangères DFAE
Secrétariat général SG-DFAE
Information DFAE

Pierre-Alain Eltschinger
Porte-parole
Palais fédéral ouest, CH-3003 Berne

1.7. Singapore:

Dear Sir

I refer to your letter dated 30 September 2012.

As indicated in Article 41 of the Vienna Convention on Diplomatic Relations, diplomats are to respect the laws and regulations of the receiving State.

The Ministry takes a serious view of diplomats who do not settle their traffic fines promptly. All Diplomatic Missions in Singapore are required to cooperate and settle all traffic fines incurred by their staff in Singapore.

The Ministry does not publish the data that you requested in your letter and is therefore unable to provide them to you.

With best regards.

WEE SOEK YEN (MS)
ASSISTANT DIRECTOR/PROTOCOL

1.8. <u>Here is another answer from Singapore:</u>

9 January 2013

Dear Sir

I refer to your letters dated 22 November 2012 and 12 December 2012 addressed to the Ministry and the Prime Minister's Office.

As explained in our letter dated 2 November 2012, the Ministry does not publish the data that you have requested for and is therefore unable to release them to you.

With best regards.

BHAVANI D/O NYANAJEGARAN (MS)
PUBLIC AFFAIRS OFFICER/PUBLIC AFFAIRS DIRECTORATE

1.9. Norway:

16 January 2013

Violation of rules of the road and parking rules by foreign diplomats in Norway.

The Ministry of Foreign Affairs refers to your letter of 12 December 2012, to the Prime Minister, regarding violation of rules of the road and parking rules by foreign diplomats in Norway.

Questions regarding the conduct of foreign diplomats in Norway are the responsibility of this Ministry, therefore we have been asked to reply to the above mentioned letter. As mentioned in our letter of 15 November 2012 in response to your letter of 30 September 2012 to the Minister of Justice, the article 41.1 of the Vienna Convention on Diplomatic Relations, states that it is the duty of all persons who enjoy privileges and immunities under the Convention to respect the laws and regulations of the receiving State. Diplomatic vehicles are subject to Norwegian parking laws and regulations, and their owners are held responsible for parking violations.

In this respect, it is the impression of this Ministry that violation of rules and regulations regarding traffic and parking is not a major problem within the diplomatic community in Norway.

Parking violations are not within the jurisdiction of this Ministry. The Ministry is therefore unfortunately not in the position to provide detailed information regarding violation of the parking regulations caused by foreign diplomats in Norway. This information is the responsibility of the municipal traffic authority of Oslo. Any further questions related to parking violations may be addressed to the following:

Kemnerkontoret I Oslo (City of Oslo Tax Collection Office)
Pilestredet 33
N-0166 Oslo

Yours faithfully

Arthur Baste Knutsen
Assistant director general

Vigdis Hansen Rosdahl
Adviser

1.10. Another answer from Norway:

15 November 2012

The violation of rules of the road and parking rules by foreign diplomats in Norway.

Dear Mr. Sergiy Novikov,

The Ministry of Foreign Affairs, Section for Diplomatic Relations refers toy your letter of 30 September 2012, which was first sent to the Ministry of Justice in Norway, regarding the violation of rules of the road and parking rules by foreign diplomats in Norway. The Ministry will draw your attention to the following.

Under article 41 of the Vienna Convention on Diplomatic Relations, it is the duty of all persons who enjoy privileges and immunities under the Convention to respect the laws and regulations of the receiving State. Diplomatic vehicles are subject to Norwegian parking laws and regulations, and their owners are held responsible for parking violations. Parking is regulated by the Traffic regulations § 17 and the Road traffic act §5. The municipal traffic authority of Oslo enforces the parking regulations in Oslo. Cf also the Ministry's publication, "Diplomat in Norway", chapter 22 and chapter 24, on the following internet page:

http://www.regjeringen.no/en/dep/ud/about_mfa/doplomatic_ relations/diplomat_no way.html?id=666838#22.

It is also the Ministry's expectation that all tickets fines related to traffic violations incurred by persons who holds diplomatic privileges are settled with the authority issuing the fine. The Ministry's policy is based on the principal equal treatment, and not on reciprocity.

Yours faithfully

Arthur Baste Knutsen
Assistant director general

Vigdis Hansen Rosdahl
Adviser

1.11. New Zealand:

14 November 2012

Dear Mr Novikov

Thank you for your letter of 30 September regarding the violation of rules of the road and parking rules by foreign diplomats in New Zealand.

All foreign diplomatic and consular staff accredited to New Zealand from another country have either diplomatic status or consular status under the two Vienna Conventions on Diplomatic and Consular Relations. These two conventions have legal effect in New Zealand through two Acts of Parliament: the Diplomatic Privileges and Immunities Act 1968 and the corresponding Consular Privileges and Immunities Act 1971.

Under Article 41 of the diplomatic convention and Article 55 of the consular convention, all those enjoying either diplomatic or consular privileges and immunities have a duty to: 'respect the laws and regulations of the receiving State.....' The New Zealand Government takes this duty very seriously with respect to traffic violations of any sort and ensures that foreign diplomats do pay any fines and address any violations without using their immunity to avoid the consequences of breaking the law.

The New Zealand Government therefore does not hold statistics of those who avoid payment of traffic fines as all those who come to the attention of the New Zealand Police and identify themselves as having diplomatic status are reported to the Ministry of Foreign Affairs and Trade for follow-up.

Yours sincerely

Hon Murray McCully
Minister of Foreign Affairs

1.12. Moldavia:

9 January 2013

Referring to your letter of September 30, 2012, about the violations of the traffic rules by the Diplomatic Corps accredited in the Republic of Moldova, I will make a small overview of the Moldovan contraventional system in respect to the diplomats.

The legislation of the Republic of Moldova, mainly art 4 of the Contraventional Code, stipulates that diplomatic agents accredited to Moldova benefit of immunities against contraventional offences.

Regulation of road safety does not make any difference between the participants to the traffic, therefore, on the basis of art. 41 of the Vienna Convention of Diplomatic Relations, the diplomats are obliged to respect the national laws and regulations.

In case a road offence is committed by a diplomat, the police initiate the contravention procedure, but do not apply the sanction. Before applying to sanction, the police inquires the Ministry of Foreign Affairs and European Integration, State Diplomatic Protocol, to confirm the privileges and immunities of the offender. After that, MFAEI informs the Embassy about the offence and requires actions to be taken, and is up to the Embassy to solve the issue with the police, in order to avoid abuses of privileges and immunities.

In some specific situations the pickup of the car license plates is applied, as a measure of constraint, when the offence committed presents a danger or a serious impediment to other participants to the traffic (speeding, illegal parking, no car insurance or technical test of the car). In these situations, the diplomatic agents have the choice whether to remedy the deficiencies and pay the fine or to wait for entire procedure mentioned above.

During year 2012 the Protocol was informed about 14 cases of traffic rules violations.

Kind regards,
Dinu Vataman
Consilier

1.13. Malaysia:

19 November 2012

ADHERENCE OF THE RULES OF THE ROAD AND PARKING RULES BY FOREIGN DIPLOMATS IN MALAYSIA

Thank you for your inquiry via letter DR4361 dated September, 30, 2012 on the adherence of the rules of the roads by foreign diplomats in Malaysia.

By and large, the Ministry notices that there are no cases of flagrant violations of traffic rules by foreign diplomats in Malaysia. Foreign diplomats in Malaysia who have been fined for traffic violations during their tour of duty have been paying their corresponding fines in good time.

The above is for your kind attention, please.

Thank you.

Yours sincerely,

(ONG TZE SHEN)
Protocol Department
p.p. Secretary General
Ministry of Foreign Affairs

1.14. Luxembourg:

Luxembourg, November 2nd 2012

Dear Sir,

Concerning your request ref DR4363 as of September 29, I regret to inform you that the Grand-Ducal Police does not establish specific statistics on violation of traffic rules by drivers with diplomatic privileges.

However, I would like to refer you to our website http://www.police.public.lu/ where you can find further information and publications which might be useful.

The Secretary General

Jean-Marie WAGNER

1.15. Liechtenstein:

5 November 2012

Dear Mr Novikov,

With reference to your letter dated 30 September 2012 regarding the violation of traffic rules by foreign diplomats in the Principality of Liechtenstein, I can inform you as follows:

All diplomats, who are accredited to the Principality of Liechtenstein, reside either in Switzerland, in Austria or in Germany. There are no foreign diplomats residing in the Principality of Liechtenstein.

Yours sincerely,

Christine Stehrenberger
Deputy Director

1.16. <u>Kazakhstan:</u>

8 November 2012

Referring to your letter ref. DR4355 as of September 30, 2012, we inform you that the data about the violations of traffic rules by the Diplomatic Corps is for official use only.
Therefore, it's impossible to submit the requested data.

M. Atamkulov
The Chief of the State Protocol Service

1.17. Ireland:

16 April, 2013

Dear Mr. Novikov,

I am directed by the Minister of Justice, Equality and Defence, Mr Alan Shatter, T.D., to refer to your correspondence dated 29 September, 2012 in relation to diplomatic privilege in the context of compliance with road traffic legislation in Ireland. The delay in replying is regretted.

The Minister is informed by An Garda Síochána (the Irish Police Force) that diplomats residing in a foreign country are protected from prosecution by the Vienna Convention of Diplomatic Relations 1961. Article 31 of the Convention states that "a diplomatic agent shall enjoy immunity from the criminal jurisdiction of the receiving state".

The Minister is also informed that the statistical information requested by you in relation to compliance with road traffic legislation by diplomats, while resident in Ireland, is not available.

Yours sincerely,

Damien Brennan
Private Secretary to the Minister for Justice and Equality

1.18. Georgia:

Mr. Sergiy,

In response to your letter of December 12, 2012 we hereby inform you that the Ministry of Internal Affairs of Georgia does not possess any statistical data concerning the violation og thr traffic rules by the individuals with the immunity provided by the Vienna Convention of Diplomatic Relations; also, no separation takes place regarding the offences participated by the persons with diplomatic status in Georgia, employees of the embassies and other international organizations. The Department of Patrol Police of the Ministry of Internal Affairs of Georgia does not apply any special or different sanctions against the above mentioned types of individuals for the offences enlisted by you.

Sincerely,

Teona Kozmanashvili

Deputy Head of the Public Information Issuance Bureau

Administrative Department

1.19. Finland:

12 October 2012

Thank you for your letter of 29 September 2012 concerning the violation of road and parking regulations by foreign diplomats and other mission staff members in Finland. Unfortunately I am not able to give you a detailed answer to your inquiry because the Ministry does not have any official statistics for these kind of infringements. Actually according to Finnish law the Ministry is not allowed to keep any criminal/police records.

I am able to tell you in general that infringements of parking regulations are obviously the most common infringements by privileged persons. Also speeding is reported occasionally to the Ministry. Cases where drunken driving is suspected come rarely to the Ministry´s knowledge.

In case you would like to have more information about parking tickets issued to mission staff members please contact the Customer Service of the Public Works Department of the City of Helsinki (rakennusvirasto@hel.fi<mailto:rakennusvirasto@hel.fi>). As regards other infringements I kindly advise you to contact the Customer Service of the Helsinki Police Deparment tel +358 71 877 4002. They will be able to tell you if any statistics are available concerning your inquiry.

With kind regards,

Sinikka Malmberg
Legal Officer
Ministry for Foreign Affairs
Protocol Services

1.20. <u>Here is another answer from the police of Finland:</u>

National　　　　　Police　　　　Board　　　　1　　　　(1)
12.2.2013 2020/2013/26
Your e-mail 12.12.2012

The violation of rules of the road rules by foreign diplomats in Finland

I am sorry I have to say that Finland is not available disaggregated data on diplomats to road traffic offenses.

Finnish police believes that diplomats rarely commit any kind of crimes.

Heikki Ihalainen
superintendent
National Police Board

1.21. Denmark:

8 November 2012

Reference is made to your letter of September 29, 2012 concerning violation of rules of the road and parking rules by foreign diplomats in Denmark.

I can inform you that all violations of Danish Traffic Acts by diplomats are followed closely by this Ministry.

In general, diplomats in Denmark are not fined for exceeding the speed limits. However, the Protocol Department will call every single case to the attention of the relevant Head of Mission.

Privileged persons in Denmark are not exempt from paying parking fees.

Please be informed that due to the need for protection of Danish foreign policy and/or of Danish external economic interests, including relations with foreign powers or international institutions, the Ministry of Foreign Affairs does not give any detailed information with regard to which diplomats or foreign diplomatic representations that violate the rules of the road or parking rules in Denmark.

Yours sincerely,
Annette Lassen

ANNETTE LASSEN
DEPUTY DIRECTOR OF PROTOCOL / MINISTER COUNSELLOR
MINISTRY OF FOREIGN AFFAIRS / PROTOCOL DEPARTMENT

1.22. Czech Republic:

30 October 2012

Dear Mr. Novikov,

With reference to your letter ref. DR4341 of 29 September 2012, I wish to inform you that the Ministry of Foreign Affairs of the Czech Republic cannot grant your request for the disclosure of information on traffic offences committed by persons enjoying privileges and immunities. The Ministry of Foreign Affairs very thoroughly monitors all violations of Czech legislation committed by such persons; however, due to certain laws and regulations as well as due to certain procedures applied by other authorities involved in administrative proceedings it is unable to keep a complete register covering all offences and offenders. Likewise, the Ministry of Foreign Affairs does not as a rule receive information about fines paid by persons enjoying privileges and immunities. The disclosure of incomplete information could lead to the formation of a highly subjective and distorted picture of the conduct of the staff of the diplomatic missions and consular posts of different states.

Sincerely yours,

Tomáš Pernický
Director of the Diplomatic Protocol

1.23. Croatia:

9 January 2013

Re: traffic violations by foreign diplomats

Dear Mr. Novikov,

Unfortunately, we cannot provide you with the requested information, simply because our Ministry of Interior does not keep that kind of evidence.

Thank you for your interest,

Best regards,
Public Relations Department
Croatian Government

1.24. Another answer from Croatia:

8 January 2013

Dear Mr Novikov,
In response to your request, we would like to inform you that the Ministry of Foreign and European Affairs does not keep records regarding the traffic and parking violations made by foreign diplomats.

Sincerely,
Public Relations Office
Ministry of Foreign and European Affairs

1.25. Brazil:

27 May 2013

Dear Mister Novikov,

The Ministry of Foreign Affairs informs that, according to current practice in Brazil, foreign diplomats are not exempt from obeying the transit rules from the receiving state. Since 2008, the fleet of diplomatic vehicles inscribed under license plates such as "CD, CC, CMD, AD and OI" are submitted to the Brazilian Traffic Code. Therefore, such vehicles do not have privileged usage, for they are subjected to fines and parking fees.

2. Fines and parking tickets are not submitted to the diplomatic proceeding, as they are sent directly to the diplomat or the mission accountable for the vehicle. For this reason, the Ministry of Foreign Affairs does not hold figures of offenses committed by foreign diplomatic agents.

Cordially,

Flávio Marcílio Moreira Sapha
Coordenação-Geral de Privilégios e Imunidades.
Ministério das Relações Exteriores

1.26. Bulgaria:

Sofia, October 23rd, 2012

Dear Mr. Novikov,

In response to your letter dated September 29th 2012 (ref. DR 4332), requesting information about violations of road traffic rules by foreign diplomats, accredited to the Republic of Bulgaria, I would like to inform you as follows:

Under the provisions of Article 41, paragraph 1 of the Vienna Convention of Diplomatic Relations of 1961, it is the duty of diplomatic agents, enjoying privileges and immunity from the jurisdiction of the receiving State, to respect the laws and regulations of the host State, including the existing traffic and parking regulations.

As to your specific inquiries, I would like to clarify that information about offences of traffic rules in the Republic of Bulgaria is available from the Ministry of Interior of the Republic of Bulgaria.

Furthermore, I would like to note that unpaid fines are within the competence of the National Revenue Agency, which has the obligation to collect outstanding payments.

At last but not least, the observance of parking rules is under the control of local municipalities.

In accordance with the Law on Access to Public Information (Prom. SG. 55/2000, last amend. SG. 39/2011), the Ministry of Foreign Affairs of the Republic of Bulgaria is not supposed to provide you with the requested information.

Yours sincerely,

Peter Obbov,
Chief of State Ceremonial Department,
Ministry of Foreign Affairs of the Republic of Bulgaria

More comments on the issue of diplomats' traffic violations given by diplomatic staff are presented below:

A Russian diplomat shares his opinion:

I work in Latin America. To the best of my knowledge, the society does not mind the actual situation.

Indeed, diplomats have immunity, i.e. are not subject to, say, inspection, deprivation of the driving right, (often) fines, etc.

What makes them violate rules? The reasons are different. Quite naturally, their awareness of their impunity is encouraging... There are boasting leaders who believe it to raise them above mere mortals, which is, of course, wrong. Yet, ministry of foreign affairs officials are mostly polite and well-cultured people; so violators are totally unwelcome.

A lot depends on the situation in the host country and whether the local government is going to overlook the problem. For instance, the Cuban police never stop cars with diplomatic number plates for mere fear. The diplomats I have met there behaved rather outrageously. In Panama, there are no front number plates, so it is not infrequent for the police to stop diplomatic cars on such common grounds as speeding, or at night, when the police arrange "roadblocks" to sobriety test every driver for. Traffic violations will make you blush and apologize. The local police is largely unaware of what a diplomatic number plate is. Sometimes you have to wait for an officer to come and clear the situation. It feels embarrassing, as if you discredited your country.

At the same time, Panamanian authorities never charge fines. In other countries, such as Nicaragua, the police try to record all violations and report them to the Embassy. The month's most notorious traffic violators are likely to suffer a showdown with their management or even have their official driving rights restricted.

The Ministry of Foreign Affairs has its own statistics. I recall a single ambassador whom a ministerial order forbade to drive because he was always crushing cars. He just was unable to drive. Quite naturally, his personal driver was having a rough time.

As for office-related necessity, receiving an important delegation is a situation in which everything is acceptable for diplomats. Speeding when late for the airport, crossing a double solid line - everything will be forgiven if committed for the sake of business; and the local authorities will help you.

Actually, Medvedev has recently removed a Russian ambassador in a Latin American country because of traffic jams that occurred during Medvedev's visit to the capital, claiming the ambassador to have been "poorly prepared" for the visit. Kremlin officials are used to having all roads blocked.

Also, many intelligence officers work in embassies under a diplomatic cover. Obviously, they are more prone to traffic violations out of necessity.

Another important and typical issue is alcohol in diplomatic work. Drinking during receptions is often part of the official duty. Naturally, many diplomats use the phenomenon to mask their alcohol addiction. At the present stage, requiring employees to go to parties by taxi on workday evenings would be unrealistic in countries with poor public safety. The ambassador is mostly the only one enjoying a personal driver.

Here is the opinion of one of the officials of the Ministry of Foreign Affairs:

i. Such diplomats' traffic violations do not have a psychological ground. Whenever a person gets a bit of freedom, he/she is happy to be able to enjoy it. It spirals with time.

ii. On embassies' struggle against such violations: Technically, it should have a disciplinary effect. Yet, such cases are actually very rare. The embassy is one team. Everybody helps his or her colleagues. Leaders tend to ignore such "pranks," which happens partly due to the fact that a supervisor can be punished for poor explanatory work with his/her subordinates' violations, too."

iii. I would like to note that diplomats are mostly well-educated people and are willing to avoid backflashing whenever possible. In any case, the work of a diplomat is primarily assessed not by his/her traffic performance but by his/her job-related achievements. Several employees have practiced serial violations, in particular, playing the sports mode. However, the main reason was that no serious sanctions were applied to them.

The second part of the present book deals with personae non grata

Usually the reason for declaring someone persona non grata is the diplomat's hostility towards the government of the host country, interference with its internal affairs, disrespect of its laws, customs, institutions, indiscretions, etc. A vague phrase "for impermissible activities incompatible with diplomatic status" often lies behind this, which can also mean a charge of espionage. No government is obliged to explain its reasons for declaring a diplomat persona non grata.

Are the countries ready to disclose the reasons? If not, what are the reasons for concealing such information?

Below, there are the official responses to the question obtained from 21 countries:

re: regarding the cases of application of Article 9 of Vienna Convention on Diplomatic Relations of 1961

According to Article 9, the state of residence can inform the sending state of a member of the diplomatic staff of the mission being persona non grata or of any other member of the mission staff being inadmissible without being obliged to motivate its decision. This procedure is usually referred to as that of renvoi in press materials.

The information concerning such a renvoi is that of public importance, and providing information of this kind meets the standards of transparency in the work of the state structures.

Please provide the following information:

1. How many decisions did the state structures of your country take in accordance with Vienna Convention on Diplomatic Relations of 1961, viz., informing of a persona non grata, informing of a staff member being inadmissible, renvoi, in years 2008, 2009, 2010, 2011, 2012.

2. Concerning diplomats* of what countries were these decisions taken by the relevant authorities of your country in the period of 2008-2012?

---

*In accordance with articles 1 and 31 of Vienna Convention on Diplomatic Relations of 1961, "members of the diplomatic staff" and "diplomatic agents" belong to diplomats uncharged with responsibility in the country of residence.

3. If you consider it possible, please provide information on motivation (reasons, circumstances) concerning at least some cases of the above mentioned decisions taken by the relevant authorities of your country in the period of 2007-2012.

The ministries of foreign affairs of 21 countries commented on this issue.

2.1. Lithuania:

10 December 2012

Regarding your enquiry we would like to kindly remind you that according to the Article 9 of Vienna Convention on Diplomatic Relations the receiving State may at any time and without having to explain its decision, notify the sending State that the head of the mission or any member of the diplomatic staff of the mission is persona non grata or that any other member of the staff of the mission is not acceptable.

Declaring a member of the diplomatic staff of the mission 'persona non grata' is an extreme diplomatic measure, which is usually handled on bilateral basis between the receiving State and the sending State. Vienna Convection does not stipulate neither the principles or scope of notification nor explanation of reasons and circumstances related to the issues of persona non grata.

Those issues are relatively rare in diplomatic practice and tend to be solved in spirit of mutual respect and understanding.

Director

Diana Grikienienè

2.2. New Zealand:

19 April 2013

Dear Mr Novikov

Thank you for your letter regarding the cases of application of Article 9 of the 1961 Vienna Convention on Diplomatic Relations, by New Zealand.

The New Zealand Government declared two foreign diplomats 'Persona Non Grata' during the period of time you have outlined in your letter. However, on both occasions it was carried out as a reciprocal measure and not as a result of any wrong doing by the foreign diplomats in question. The details of these cases are confidential to the Government so it is not possible to provide the comprehensive response you seek to question 3.

Yours sincerely,

Hon Murray McCully
Minister of Foreign Affairs

2.3. Norway:

25 February 2013

Information Requested on the Vienna Convention on Diplomatic Relations

Reference is made to your letter dated 26 November 2012 addressed to the Prime Minister of Norway. The letter has been forwarded to the Ministry of Foreign Affairs.

In your letter, you request information on how many decisions Norway has taken in accordance with the Vienna Convention on Diplomatic Relations in the years 2008-2012 regarding persons being declared "persona non grata". Furthermore, you want to know which countries the possible decisions concerned and information on the motivation for the possible decisions.

According to Article 9 of the Vienna Convention on Diplomatic Relations of 1961 "The receiving State may at any time and without having to explain its decision, notify the sending State that the head of the mission or any member of the diplomatic staff of the mission is persona non grata or that any other member of the staff of the mission is not acceptable. [...]"

For Norway, as for most states, declaring a member of the diplomatic staff of a foreign mission persona non grata, is only occasionally deemed necessary. Concerns the receiving State may have regarding members of other States' missions, can be resolved in many different ways. This is the nature of diplomacy.

On a few occasions, Norway has declared diplomatic staff of missions persona non grata. Norway considers any notifications of such a decision to be part of the privileged communication between States. Detailed information is usually not made public.

According to our archives, the Ministry has not given any public statements during the years 2008-2012 concerning possible decisions to declare diplomatic staff persona non grata. For this reason the Ministry is not able to provide you with information as requested in your letter.

Regards

Kristian Jervell
Deputy Director General

Kristina Nygård
Adviser

2.4. <u>Slovenia:</u>

20 December 2012

With reference to your questions (letter ref. DR7787 of 22 November 2012) concerning the application of the Article 9 of Vienna Convention on Diplomatic Relations of 1961 by the Republic of Slovenia, we inform you that on 31 May 2012 Slovenia decided to declare the Vienna based Syrian Ambassador to Slovenia persona non grata. The decision was based on principled positions on the alarming situation following the outbreak of the crisis in Syria. Slovenia condemned the escalating brutal violence and systematic violations of human rights.

Feel free to contact us for any additional information.

Sincerely,
REPUBLIKA SLOVENIJA
MINISTRSTVO ZA ZUNANJE ZADEVE

2.5. Republic of South Africa:

14 March 2013

We refer to your letter ref: DR79035 dated 22 November 2012 which was addressed to the Office of the President of South Africa.

The responses to your questions are provided as follows:

1. Response to question 1

There were no accredited members of the diplomatic and consular community that were declared as persona non grata in accordance with the Vienna Convention on Diplomatic Relations of 1961, for the mentioned years of 2008, 2009, 2010, 2011 and 2012.

2. Response to question 2

Not applicable

3. Response to question 3

Not applicable.

In the past the Government of South Africa has opted to allow the sending state to deal with few cases of misdemeanors committed by accredited members of the diplomatic and consular community without having to invoke article 9 of the Vienna Convention on Diplomatic Relations of 1961.

With kind regards

Simphiwe Magida (Mr)
Deputy-Director

Branch: State Protocol
Directorate: Diplomatic Immunities and Priveleges
Subdirectorate: Diplomatic Security, Immunity Disputes Permits & Front Office
OR Tambo Building
Room NEB2B -G-089
460 Soutpansberg Road
Rietondale, 0184
Private Bag X 152
Pretoria
0001

2.6. Sweden:

11 March 2013

Written communications to the Ministry for Foreign Affairs - request for information on traffic offences, etc.
(Re: Your communications dated 30 September, 22 November and 12 December 2012).

In the abovementioned communications, you made a number of requests for information that can be summarised as follows:

1.The number of cases of offences committed by diplomats in Sweden against certain traffic regulations and the number of cases of diplomats having parked illegally during the periods stated. Which countries/diplomats have not been reported for such offences?

2.The number of decisions to declare diplomats persona non grata during the periods stated.

The following can be said concerning the number of illegally parked vehicles. The Ministry regularly receives a certain amount of information about illegally parked vehicles. However, a large number of parking enforcement companies do not report illegally parked vehicles to the Ministry. Therefore, we cannot draw any certain conclusions about numbers of illegally parked vehicles.

The Ministry does not have any overall information concerning traffic offences.

The Ministry for Foreign Affairs' operations and contacts with foreign embassies here in Sweden are expected to remain confidential. The rules on secrecy in such operations are intended to protect international cooperation. Making public the details of which individuals have been declared persona non grata may be considered to interfere with Sweden's international relations. We are therefore not at liberty to make any further comments concerning your questions on this matter.

Yours sincerely,

Klas Nyman
Director

2.7. Switzerland:

6 December 2012

Dear Sir,

Thank you for your letter dated November 22, 2012.

As you mentioned, article 9, Vienna Convention 1961, allows the State of residence to declare a member of a diplomatic mission persona non grata without having to motivate its decision. It means that the State of residence has in this matter a discretionary power. Due to the fact that we are in presence of a discretionary power whose use has not to be motivated and due to the fact that the data concerning the persons who might have been concerned by the application of this provision are under personal data protection, we are not in a position to answer to your questions.

Best regards,

Carole Wälti

DFAE - DÉPARTEMENT FÉDÉRAL DES AFFAIRES ÉTRANGÈRES

Carole Wälti
Spokeperson

2.8. Great Britain:

02 January 2013

Dear Mr Novikov,

Freedom of Information Request: Ref: 1233-12

Thank you for your Freedom of Information request of 22 November asking for information about diplomatic staff being declared persona non grata, specifically:

*"1. How many decisions did the state structures of your country take in accordance with Vienna Convention on Diplomatic Relations of 1961, viz., informing of a **persona non grata,** informing of a staff member being inadmissible, renvoi, in years 2008, 2009, 2010, 2011, 2012.*

2. Concerning diplomats of what countries were these decisions taken by the relevant authorities of your country in the period of 2008-2012?

3. If you consider it possible, please provide information on motivation (reasons, circumstances) concerning at least some cases of the above mentioned decisions taken by the relevant authorities of your country in the period 2008-2012."

From our preliminary search I can confirm that the Foreign and Commonwealth Office holds information which falls within the description specified in your request. However, some of the information which we hold and which is relevant to your request is, in our view, already reasonably accessible to you. Under Section 21 (Information Accessible by Other Means) of the Freedom of Information Act, we are not required to provide information in response to a request

if it is already reasonably accessible to the applicant. Every year the Secretary of State for Foreign and Commonwealth Affairs makes a Written Ministerial Statement to Parliament on serious offences which have allegedly been committed by members of the diplomatic community in the United Kingdom. The last statement was made on 5 July 2012, and a record can be found here:
http://www.publications.parliament.uk/pa/cm201213/cmhansrd/cm120705/wmstext/120705m0001.htm.

You can also search the UK Parliament website for the Written Ministerial Statements for 2008, 2009 and 2010.

The Foreign Secretary will make a further Written Ministerial Statement in 2013, covering alleged offences in 2012. This information is therefore exempt under Section 22 of the Freedom of Information Act (Information intended for future publication). Section 22 provides that:

Information is exempt information if:

(a) the information is held by the public authority with a view to its publication, by the authority or any other person, at some future date (whether determined or not)

(b) it is reasonable in all the circumstances that the information should be withheld from disclosure until the date referred to in paragraph (a).

The exemption under Section 22 of the Freedom of Information Act recognises that it must be reasonable in all the circumstances to withhold the information until the date of publication. Given the necessary preparation and administration involved in publishing the information, we consider that our publication timetable is reasonable.

I recognise that the Foreign Secretary's annual Written

Ministerial Statement does not specify which of these alleged offences led to a diplomat being withdrawn. And there are of course other reasons why a diplomat might be withdrawn from the UK, such as a break in diplomatic relations. However, we estimate that the cost of searching for this information and complying with your request in full would exceed the appropriate limit of £600.

Section 12 of the Freedom of Information Act makes provisions for public authorities to refuse requests for information where the cost of dealing with them would exceed the appropriate limit. The limit has been specified in the Freedom of Information and Data Protection (Appropriate Limit and Fees) Regulations 2004. For central government the appropriate limit is set at £600. This represents the estimated cost of one or more persons spending $3^1/_2$ days working days in determining whether the Department holds the information, and locating, retrieving and extracting it. Your request as presently formulated is widely-framed and I estimate that it will take more than $3^1/_2$ working days to locate, retrieve and extract this information. In these circumstances we are not obliged under the Act to comply with your request.

In order for your request to fall within the appropriate limit we would recommend you narrow your request down by identifying specific subject areas outlined in your letter, which you would like us to pursue further. However, you should be aware that this does not guarantee an automatic release, as all information must be assessed in detail. Any reformulated request will be treated as a fresh request under the Act.

If you are unhappy with the service you have received in relation to your request and wish to make a complaint or *request an internal review, you should contact the Information Rights Team at dp-foi.img@fco.gov.uk. Please note any request for an internal review must be submitted within 40 working days from the date our response was issued.*

If you are not content with the outcome of the internal review, you may apply directly to the Information Commissioner for a decision. Generally, the ICO cannot make a decision unless you have exhausted the complaints procedure provided by the Foreign & Commonwealth Office.

The Information Commissioner can be contacted at: The Information Commissioner's Office, Wycliffe House, Water Lane, Wilmslow, Cheshire SK9 5AF.

Yours sincerely,
Diplomatic Missions and International Organisations Unit
Protocol Directorate

2.9. <u>Ukraine</u>:

30 January 2013

Dear Mr. Novikov,

The Security service has considered your appeal to the President of Ukraine, directed to us by the Ministry of Foreign Affairs of Ukraine.

We inform you that according to the records of the Security service of Ukraine in the period from 2008 to 2012 of the Ministry of Foreign Affairs of Ukraine, several diplomatic representatives of foreign countries were announced to be "persona non grata" for the activities incompatible with their diplomatic status and powers, fixed by the Vienna Convention on Diplomatic Relations of 1961.

Since the mentioned question concerns the bilateral relations between Ukraine and other countries, the diplomatic practice makes no provision for uncovering such information to third parties.

P. Shatkovskyi
First Vice-President of the Head

2.10. Bosnia and Herzegovina:

21 December 2012

The Ministry of Foreign Affairs of Bosnia and Herzegovina has received your request relating to the declaration of undesirable persons with diplomatic status and forwarded it to the Presidency of Bosnia and Herzegovina which has competent jurisdiction to decide on this matter.

The Ministry of Foreign Affairs of Bosnia and Herzegovina participates in the process of considering the status of persons with diplomatic status, but a formal decision on declaring someone to be persona non grata is made by the Presidency of Bosnia and Herzegovina, which can give information about it to the public.

Mayors office

Regoje Nebojša
Minister-Counsellor

2.11. Ireland:

13 December 2012

Dear Mr. Novikov,

On behalf of the Tanaiste and Minister for Foreign Affairs and Trade, Mr Eamon Gilmore, T.D., I wish to refer to your letter of 22nd November 2012.

On two occasions during the period you referred to, 2008 - 2012, the Irish Government has asked a sending state to withdraw a member of diplomatic staff accredited to Ireland. In this context, I would refer you to Press Releases dated 15/06/2010 and 1/02/2011, available on my Department's website at http://www.dfa.ie/home/index.aspx?id=379.

You will wish to note that it would not be usual to provide those names in keeping with normal diplomatic practice.

Yours sincerely,

Mary Connery
Private Secretary

2.12. Georgia:

30 December 2013

The Ministry of Foreign Affairs of Georgia acknowledges the receipt of your letter dated 22 November, 2012 and is pleased to inform you on the following:

Georgia is a state party to the 1961 Vienna Convention on Diplomatic Relations and fulfills its obligations in good faith and full compliance with the provisions prescribed by the Convention.

Since the reestablishment of the Georgian statehood in 1992, there has been no practice of declaring a foreign diplomatic agent persona non grata by Georgia. Moreover as the practice of the other States unveils, there is generally no formal procedure to be carried out in case of declaring a diplomatic agent as incompatible with his/her status. In many occasions, the Foreign Ministries based on the decision of the Head of the Government send the pertinent notification to the other States diplomatic mission or a governmental body on the matter.

The above practice falls into full compliance with Article 9 of the Convention, which does not provide for an obligation of any State Party to communicate the reasons on which it bases its decision regarding the notification sent to the other state that the head of the mission or any member of the diplomatic staff of the mission is deemed to be a persona non grata or that any other member of the staff of the mission is declared not acceptable. Furthermore, the said Article does not prescribe any rule or procedure in accordance to which the notification on the persona non grata should be provided to the other party.

The Ministry of Foreign Affairs would like to hereby emphasize that the national legislation of Georgia does not envisage any provision regarding the above-mentioned issue. Hence the rule prescribed in Article 9 of the Convention is of a self-executive character in relation to the legislation of Georgia.

Respectfully,

Press and Information Department
Ministry of Foreign Affairs of Georgia

2.13. Finland:

19 December 2012

Reference: Your letter of 22 November 2012 concerning request for information

As a reply to your inquiry I would like to inform you that it is not possible to give you detailed information about the individual cases where the Ministry for Foreign Affairs has declared a foreign diplomat or a staff member of a foreign mission persona non grata or otherwise inadmissable.

This is because these documents concern the relationship of Finland with a foreign state and access to these documents could damage or compromise Finland's international relations or its ability to participate in international co-operation (Section 24, subparagraph 2 of the Act on the Openness of Government Activities).

You can request for an official decision of the Ministry for Foreign Affairs in this matter if you so wish. The official decision of the Ministry is appealable.

With kind regards,

Sinikka Malmberg
Legal Officer
Ministry for Foreign Affairs

2.14. Germany:

20 December 2012

Your request addressed to the Chancellor on 22 November this year was handed to me for reply.

The federal government has made a certain use in the past out of the right under the Article 9 of the Vienna Convention on Diplomatic Relations and reserves this right in the future explicitly.

As you know from the press, 4 Syrian diplomats were declared and recognized by Article 9 of the Vienna Convention on Diplomatic Relations personas non grata recently. This expulsion was politically motivated. It served the protests and the demarcation of the current regime in Syria. Politically motivated acts are distinguished from the rule and are often coordinated internationally in order to achieve maximum political impact. The situation is different with expulsion being a last diplomatic mean caused by serious misconduct of a foreign diplomat, for example, by substantial and repeated violations of the local law. In general, however, the two countries are concerned in seeking solutions in the statement below, which at least not permanently affect relations. The dismissal by the sending country at the request of the host country would be considered as such means.

Unfortunately, I cannot provide any statistical evidence available on this topic. So I hope to have helped you with this information.

Sincerely yours,

Gisbert Bruns

2.15. Denmark:

21 December 2012

Re: Application of Article 9 of the Vienna Convention on Diplomatic Relation

Dear Mr. Novikov,

Thank you for your letter of 22 November 2012 in which you enquire about the number and nationalities of diplomat in Denmark being declared 'persona non grata' in accordance with Article 9 of the Vienna Convention on Diplomatic Relations during the five year period 2008-2012 and about the motivation for any such declarations of 'persona non grata'.

Denmark has applied Article 9 in three (3) instances in 2011 whereby three diplomats were declared 'persona non grata'. We have had no reasons to bring the Article into use in 2008, 2009, 2010 or 2012.

As you will understand and appreciate from prior correspondence with our Ministry we cannot offer you information on the nationalities of the abovementioned three people or the motivation for declaring them 'persona non grata'. The reason is the need for protection of Danish foreign policy and/or of Danish external economic interests, including relations with foreign powers or international institutions.

Yours sincerely,
Søren Særmark-Thomsen

2.16. Cuba:

30 April 2013

CENTER
PRESS
INTERNATIONAL
Ministry of Foreign Affairs

Havana, April 17, 2013
"Year 55 of the Revolution"

We respond to this letter to the Ministry of Foreign Affairs of the Republic of Cuba, dated November 22, 2012, requesting information on the implementation of Article 9 of the Vienna Convention on Diplomatic Relations of 1961 by the Republic of Cuba, concerning the statement of the diplomatic staff as persona non grata.

In connection with that case, I can state that in the period from 2008 to present, the Ministry of Foreign Affairs did not declare any foreign diplomat accredited to the Republic of Cuba persona non grata.

Sincerely,
International Press Centre

2.17. Czech Republic:

11 January 2013

Dear Mr. Novikov,

With reference to your letter ref. DR7703 of 22 November 2012, I wish to inform you that the Ministry of Foreign Affairs of the Czech Republic does not, as a rule, publish its decisions whereby a member of a foreign diplomatic mission accredited to the territory of the Czech Republic is declared persona non grata or unacceptable. Both situations are, by nature, highly exceptional. The declaration is subject to reciprocity and can be made only in the event of an extremely grave violation of Czech legislation or other unacceptable interference with the Czech Republic's interests. The Vienna Convention on Diplomatic Relations itself respects the special nature of decisions declaring a person persona non grata or unacceptable and grants the receiving state the right not to explain the reasons for the decision.

Sincerely yours,

Tomáš Pernický
Director of the Diplomatic Protocol

2.18. Canada:

21 December 2012

We received your letter (Ref: DR5717, dated November 22, 2012). Here are our responses:

The decision by Canada to declare a foreign representative persona non grata, in accordance with the established international norm based on the Vienna Convention on Diplomatic Relations (article 9), is a rare occurrence.

We do not typically comment publicly on the specifics of decisions to seek the recall of a foreign diplomatic agent or a member of his or her family, including the names and countries of origin of the individuals.

Only in specific circumstances have we chosen to comment on this; see for example:

regarding **Iran***:*

http://www.international.gc.ca/media/aff/news-communiques/2012/09/07a.aspx?lang=eng&view=d

and **Syria***:*

http://www.international.gc.ca/media/aff/news-communiques/2012/05/29a.aspx?view=d

Regards,

Ian Trites
Spokesperson | Porte-parole
Media Relations | Service des relations avec les medias

2.19. <u>Columbia</u>:

Bogotá, March 12, 2013

Subject: Response Communication of 22 November 2013

Mr. Novikov:

In response to your letter of November 22, 2012 and as stipulated clearly in Article 9 of the Vienna Convention of 1961, the receiving state, without having to give reasons for its decision, may notify the sending state of its decision to consider the head of mission or any other staff member to be persona non grata. Therefore, in the case of a unilateral and sovereign decision of each state, it is not possible to report what have happened and to publish the reasons that led to a decision in this regard. In the records of the Directorate General of Protocol established that during the years 2008 - 2012 has been declared to Colombia as an accredited diplomat persona non grata.

Sincerely yours,

ALEXANDER POTDEVIN GUTIERREZ
Coordinator of Internal Working Group of Privileges and Immunities

2.20. <u>Here is another response from Columbia:</u>

7 February 2013

I hereby make reference to your letter dated 22 November 2013, received on 31 January by the International Legal Affairs Division of the Ministry of Foreign Affairs of the Republic of Colombia, by which you requested data concerning declarations of persona non grata issued by the Republic of Colombia between 2008 and 2012. In this regard, I respectfully inform that your request was transferred to the Protocol Office of this Ministry due to its legal competence over the matter.

The referred transference proceeds on the basis of article 10 (7) of Decree No 3355 of 7th September 2009, and article 2 of Resolution 5813 of 16th November of 2011.

Kind regards

Giovanny Vega Barbosa
Coordinador
Grupo Interno de Trabajo Consultivo y Extradición
Dirección de Asuntos Jurídicos Internacionales
Ministerio de Relaciones Exteriores

2.21. Belarus:

13 December 2012

Dear Mr.Sergei Novikov,

Under the Article 9 of the Vienna Convention on Diplomatic Relations of 1961 and the established international practice the state has the right not to inform on the reasons of declaring a foreign citizen persona non grata.

A similar approach is used in reference to the information about the above mentioned personas provided upon the request of any individuals, including foreign citizens.

Head of the Information Department-
Press – secretary of the MFA

Mr. Andrei Savinikh

2.22. Australia:

14 December 2012

Dear Mr Novikov,

I refer to your correspondence dated 8 December 2012, in which you write:

1.How many decisions did the state structures of your country take in accordance with Vienna Convention on Diplomatic Relations of 1961, viz informing of a persona non grata, informing of a staff member being inadmissible, renvoi, in years 2008, 2009, 2010, 2011, 2012.

2.Concerning diplomats of what countries were these decisions taken by the relevant authorities of your country in the period of 2008-2012?

3.If you consider it possible, please provide information on motivation (reasons, circumstances) concerning at least some cases of the above mentioned decisions taken by the relevant authorities of your country in the period of 2008-2012.

The Freedom of Information Act (FOI Act) is available at: http://www.austlii.edu.au/au/legis/cth/consol_act/foia1982222/), and is predicated on requests for documents held by agencies.

In its current form, the scope of your request does not fall within the FOI Act as it is a request for information, rather than for documents. Section 15 (2)(b) of the FOI Act requires that requests provide such information concerning the document as is reasonably necessary to enable a responsible officer of the agency to identify it. In order for your request to proceed, you would need to re-phrase it in terms of a request for certain documents held by the Department of Foreign Affairs & Trade.

Please note that the timeframe for completing an FOI request usually takes a minimum of 30 days, and can take additional time depending on the complexity of the request and the number of relevant documents identified in our searches. Applicants who are not seeking information directly related to themselves are also liable to pay charges, which are determined on the basis of the number and complexity of the documents identified.

Also, the information you can receive under FOI is limited. In particular, if you are seeking access to information provided to the Department by someone other than you, we are required to consult with that person before releasing their information to you. The FOI Act provides that an agency is obliged to consult with third parties giving him/her the opportunity to voice their concerns on the release of that information. This does not confer the right ofveto on the release of that information. The Department's decision-maker will, however, take into consideration those concerns when making their decision.

Should you have any queries regarding this matter please respond by email to foi@dfat.gov.au or by letter to the address below.

Yours sincerely

David Yardley
Director
Freedom of Information Section
Domestic Legal Branch

The actual reasons for declaring persona non grata may vary from espionage to improper transportation of a child, who cannot get to homeland other than in the trunk of a diplomatic car.

However, ministries of foreign affairs do not appear eager to disclose any information on the countries represented by those diplomats they "kindly ask" to withdraw.

NOTES

We greatly appreciate when our readers take time to submit good reviews for our books.*

* www.amazon.com/dp/1530794048

The latest version of the book in **electronic** form can be found at the following locations:

in the **United States & Canada**:
www.amazon.com/gp/product/B015L2UOR0

in **UK** & other **European countries**:
www.amazon.co.uk/gp/product/B015L2UOR0

The latest version of the book in a **hard** copy can be found at the following locations:

in the **United States & Canada**:
www.createspace.com/6172989
www.amazon.com/dp/1530794048

in **UK** & other **European countries**:
www.createspace.com/6172989
www.amazon.co.uk/dp/1530794048